GEOGRAPHY CORNER

Rainforests

Ruth Thomson

WAYLAND

Explore the world with **Popcorn** - your complete first non-fiction library.

Look out for more titles in the Popcorn range. All books have the same format of simple text and striking images. Text is carefully matched to the pictures to help readers to identify and understand key vocabulary. www.waylandbooks.co.uk/popcorn

Published in 2013 by Wayland
Copyright © Wayland

Wayland
Hachette Children's Books
338 Euston Road
London NW1 3BH

Wayland Australia
Level 17/207 Kent Street
Sydney NSW 2000

 Produced for Wayland by
White-Thomson Publishing Ltd
www.wtpub.co.uk
+44 (0)843 208 7460

Editor: Steve White-Thomson
Designer: Clare Nicholas
Picture researcher: Ruth Thomson/Steve White-Thomson
Series consultant: Kate Ruttle
Design concept: Paul Cherrill

British Library Cataloguing in Publication Data
Thomson, Ruth, 1949-
   Rainforests. -- (Geography corner)(Popcorn)
   1. Rain forests--Juvenile literature.
   I. Title II. Series
   910.9'152-dc22

ISBN: 978 0 7502 7200 1

Wayland is a division of Hachette Children's Books,
an Hachette UK company.
www.hachette.co.uk

Printed and bound in China

Picture Credits: **Dreamstime**: Pbchaves 4, Samchad 5, Tommygun714 5, Tony1 7, Spaceheater 9, Orionmystery 9, The_guitar_mann 12-13, Smithore 15, Javarman 16, Zhu_zhu 17, Aprescindere 19, Pedro2009 20, Looby 22, Juliengrondin 22, Deriufra 22, Design56 22, Koszivu 22, Kesu01 22; **Neil Thomson**: Neil Thomson 23; **Photolibrary**: Loren McIntyre 21; **Shutterstock**: Juriah Mosin (cover), clearviewstock 8-9, Dr. Morley Read 10, glen gaffney 1/11, Mikael Damkier 13, Irishman 14; **WTPix** 2/18.

Illustrations on pages 5 and 6 by Stefan Chabluk.

 Contents

What is a rainforest?

Rainforests grow where the sun is hot
and it rains hard every day of the year.
Trees grow tall and close together
in this warm, wet climate.

There are always plenty of fruits, seeds, nuts and leaves for monkeys and other animals to eat.

Rainforests are found only near the Equator. The Equator is the line on a world map that marks the middle of the Earth.

There are different sorts of plants and animals in the rainforests of each continent.

The Amazon rainforest is the biggest rainforest in the world.

Tree frog

NORTH AMERICA

EUROPE

ASIA

AFRICA

Equator

Amazon Rainforest

SOUTH AMERICA

AUSTRALIA

Cayman

Gorilla

Rainforest layers

A rainforest has four layers where different sorts of plants and animals live.

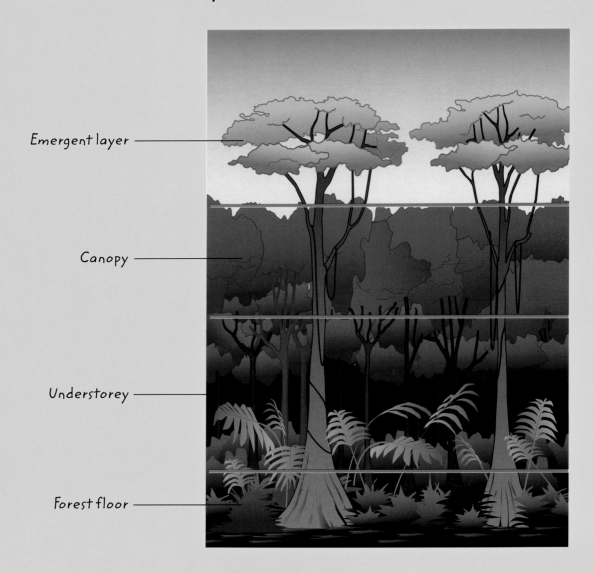

Emergent layer

Canopy

Understorey

Forest floor

Most trees only have roots underground. The giant trees in the rainforest have wide roots that grow up the trunk to keep them upright.

These wide roots are called buttress roots.

7

The forest floor

The forest floor is dark and smelly. Rotting leaves and tree trunks cover the earth.

Ferns and fungi both grow on the shady forest floor.

Many rainforest plants are unique. They may be useful for medicines.

Ants, beetles and creepy crawlies live under the leaves and in the rotten wood. Wild pigs and deer feed on fallen fruits, seeds and leaves.

Weaver ant

Goliath bird-eating spider

The understorey

The understorey is the layer above the forest floor. Small trees, such as banana trees and palm trees, grow here. They are shaded by taller trees above.

Understorey plants have large leaves to catch the dim sunlight.

Animals that are good at climbing, such as tree snakes and the clouded leopard, live in the understorey.

The clouded leopard grips branches with its sharp claws.

The canopy

Many trees grow tall to reach sunlight.
Their long trunks have only leafy branches
at the top. The treetops touch to form
a roof, called a canopy, over the forest.

The canopy keeps out most of the light to plants below.

Rainforest trees are mostly evergreens. This means they keep their tough, dark leaves all year round.

The leaves have pointy tips, so rain can fall off them easily.

drip tip

13

Canopy plants

Some plants grow on the high tree branches in the canopy. Here, sunlight can reach them. Their dangling roots take in water from falling rain.

Some branches are completely covered with plants.

Climbing plants called lianas twist around tree trunks. They grow quickly up to the canopy to find light.

Lianas loop themselves between branches.

15

Canopy animals

Animals in the canopy are good at climbing, clinging or leaping. They rarely come down from the treetops, because they can always find leaves, fruits or nuts to eat.

Orang-utans swing from the trees with their long arms.

It is noisy in the canopy. Birds and monkeys cannot see far through the thick leaves in the treetops, so they call out loudly to each other.

Macaws have strong beaks, which they use to crack hard nutshells.

People of the rainforest

People have lived in the rainforest for a long time. They use plants for food, building homes, clothes and cures for illnesses. They hunt and eat wild pigs, snakes and birds.

This boy has caught an anaconda, a snake that lives on river banks.

Some people clear small plots of land to grow food. They move every few years when the soil loses its goodness.

This woman has collected nuts to sell. First she cracks their hard shells.

Rainforests in danger

People are cutting down millions of trees. Some use the trees for timber. Others want land for cattle farms, growing crops or for mining.

Many animals and plants are becoming rare, because their homes have been cleared away.

Once trees have gone, rain washes away the soil.

The Earth needs rainforests.
The trees help to keep the air
all around the world clean.

Rainforest people,
animals and birds
need their homes.

Rainforest foods

All these food plants come from the rainforest. Have you eaten any of them? Choose one of the foods and find out how it grows.

bananas

ginger

coconuts

avocados

papayas

cinnamon

Make a model rainforest

Make a mini-rainforest in a shoebox.

You will need:

- a shoebox
- scissors and glue
- paint and paintbrush
- white and coloured card
- felt-tip pens

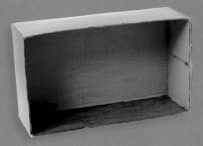

1. Paint the shoebox inside and out.

2. Cut tree trunks and leaves from coloured card.

3. Cut a slit in each trunk to make two flaps. Glue the leaves to the trunks.

4. Make some card animals. Colour them in.

5. Glue the animals on to the trees. Glue the flaps of the trees to the box base.

Glossary

climate the usual sort of weather in an area

continent one of the large areas of land that make up the Earth

dim not very clear and bright

emergent layer trees that grow taller and wider than the trees of the canopy

Equator the line on a world map that marks the middle of the Earth

evergreen evergreen plants are ones that do not lose their leaves in winter

fungi plants with no leaves, like mushrooms

mining digging something like coal or gold out of the ground

plot a small piece of land

timber wood used for building things

unique the only one of its kind

Index